COASTERS OF
THE 1950s
by
Bernard McCall

INTRODUCTION

I have searched in vain for a suitable definition of the word "classic". I have come to the conclusion that it is almost an emotional word used to describe the things with which we were familiar in our formative years and which we therefore remember with a particular fondness. I say this because there are many ship enthusiasts who would use the word "classic" to describe the coasters of the 1950s. As far as coastal shipping is concerned, the 1950s were years of rapid expansion as countries in Europe recovered from the ravages of war and there was a growing demand for the transport of raw materials as well as finished goods. Shipbuilders had full order books. In 1955, there were 56 shipyards at work in the Netherlands. The yards in some countries began to realise the virtues of series production of standard designs so we see the "Caroliner" design from Danish yards and the various standard types from J J Sietas in Germany. I have taken the opportunity in some captions to say a few words about the history of the shipyard, especially if it is one not generally known.

These were also the years when ships were owned by families. As a young ship enthusiast in the 1960s, I was fascinated by the names of the coasters. The Germans tended to favour family members - I would wonder what **Thyra Behrens** looked like in real life. The Dutch coasters were especially noteworthy with their use of exotic place names (**Mount Everest** - and even **Port Talbot**!) and Latin qualities (**Audacia**) or phrases (**Vindicat atque polit, Hoc vinces**). I sometimes wonder if it was a fascination with those Latin names that encouraged my eventual pursuit of that language to degree level - but that's another story. The names of British coasters somehow lacked the same magic. "Oh, no; not another ....*ity*". Living in Lancashire and unlikely to visit the Thames or north-east of England, I did wonder about the identity of **Dame Caroline Haslett** or **Falconer Birks**, but these were only names in an Ian Allan "spotting" book.

There is not enough space in some captions to give the whole story of a particular ship or design. Of significant interest, for example, are the German coasters of the early 1950s. On 26 September 1946, the Allied Control Council allowed the Germans to build a series of coastal vessels that should be no longer than 110 feet (33,5 metres) and with engines up to 300bhp. In 1948, the government of West Germany decided to spend DM4 million on building as many coasters as possible. A group of experts, under the direction of shipbuilding engineer Adolf Weselmann, made blueprints for a coaster design conforming to the specifications laid down by the Allied Control Council and as economically as possible. A first series of 14 ships was built between 1949 and 1951. A total of 96 ships were built to the Weselmann design.

In the pages of this book, I have used some images which show the ships in their original form and others which show them in later years, sometimes after being modified. There are one or two examples of the same ship in both guises.

As always in these books, there are sincere thanks to be offered. Firstly, I thank the many photographers who have gladly made their valued colour slides available for reproduction. I also wish to record my gratitude to the many friends who have been so willing to answer questions and solve mysteries which often arise when trying to trace ships' histories. Dag Bakka Jr, Klaus-Peter Kiedel, Bert Kruidhof, Bent Mikkelsen, and Jerzy Swieszkowski have all provided special help. Iain McCall has cast an expert eye over the text and, as always, Gil Mayes has checked several drafts of the book and willingly shared his immense knowledge. Any errors that remain are mine. Thanks also go to the Amadeus Press for their customary excellence in printing the book.

Bernard McCall   Portishead, September 2008

Published by Bernard McCall, 400 Nore Road, Portishead, Bristol, BS20 8EZ, England. Website : www.coastalshipping.co.uk
Telephone/fax : 01275 846178. E-mail : bernard@coastalshipping.co.uk
All distribution enquiries should be addressed to the publisher.

Printed by Amadeus Press, Ezra House, West 26 Business Park, Cleckheaton, West Yorkshire, BD19 4TQ
Telephone : 01274 863210; fax : 01274 863211; e-mail : info@amadeuspress.co.uk; website : www.amadeuspress.co.uk

ISBN : 978-1-902953-37-3

Front cover : There could be many candidates for the title of "classic" design but the Dutch-built coasters typified by the **John Mitchell** (384grt/58) would be strong contenders for such a title. She was built at the Hijlkema & Zonen shipyard at Martenshoek on the Winschoterdiep, a waterway long renowned for the building of splendid coasters. She was launched on 21 November 1957 and completed on 10 February 1958. Originally named **Speranza**, she was owned in Groningen and managed by N. V. Carebeka, a company which operated a large number of coasters. In May 1972, she was sold to H R Mitchell & Sons Ltd, and was renamed **John Mitchell**. This company's coasters were often used in the explosives trade and when photographed leaving Barry on 19 May 1974, she was transhipping explosives to and from a larger vessel anchored in Barry Roads. In late 1984, she was sold for scrap and on 25 January 1985 she arrived at Milton Creek, Sittingbourne, where demolition began in April 1985.

Back Cover : Many coasters built during the 1950s were eventually sold to owners in the Mediterranean after their days of trading in northern Europe were over. It was usual for the new owners to replace the original derricks with a crane which would be ideal for handling the bulk cargoes which they generally carried. The **Georgia II** (GRC, 497grt/55) was built by Stader Schiffswerft where she was launched on 3 August 1955 as **Hans Oltmann** for Johannes (Hans) Oltmann, of nearby Dornbusch, to whom she was delivered on 1 October 1955. Sold within Germany in 1970, she was renamed **Esteufer**. It was in 1974 that she headed for the Mediterranean, being renamed **Mike II** and later becoming **Athanasios II** (1976), **Olympos** (1982) and **Georgia II** in 1992. She was photographed against a characteristically Greek background at Tinos as she discharged to a single lorry on 22 December 1997. Renamed **Dimitris K** in 2003, she was scrapped at Aliaga where she arrived on 12 July 2004.

(Both photographs by Nigel Jones)

The ships of Belfast-based John Kelly Ltd were a familiar sight in the coal trades and, amongst other nicknames, they were often known as "Kelly's Coal Boats". The family-owned company dated back to the late 19th century and its ships were identified by the "Bally" prefix in their names in the latter half of the 20th century. In the 1970s, four ships were bought from Stephenson Clarke Ltd and the last of these, acquired in 1976, was the **Ballycastle** (1748grt/59). She was built by the Grangemouth Dockyard Co Ltd, launched on 24 February 1959, and handed over as **Cowdray** to Stephenson Clarke Ltd four months later. After fifteen years service in the Kelly fleet, she was sold to Lebanese owners in 1981 and was renamed **Aref**. eventually being scrapped at Eleusis in Greece in mid-1986. She was photographed in the lock at Sharpness on 31 March 1979, outward bound to Warrenpoint with a cargo of barley.

(Cedric Catt)

The decade after the end of the Second World War saw huge changes in British industry with many services and utilities being nationalised. The British Electricity Authority was established on 1 April 1948 and not only began to upgrade the system of power generating stations but also the fleet of ships that served them. Brighton B power station was commissioned in 1952 and four ships were built to serve this. The **Sir John Snell** (2947grt/55) was the third of these four. She was built by Hall, Russell and Co Ltd at Aberdeen and was launched on 11 January 1955. By the time of her delivery in August 1955, the British Electricity Authority had become the Central Electricity Authority. She was involved in one serious incident during her career when she collided with the **Lisbeth M** near the North Goodwin lightship on 4 April 1957, with the tragic loss of some crew members from

the latter ship. The ship was near the end of her career when seen passing Penarth outward bound from Cardiff on 8 May 1979. She was sold in 1980 to the Agmar Shipping Co Ltd, of Sunderland, and renamed **Agmar I** but this seems to have been only for a delivery voyage to shipbreakers. After a period laid up at Newcastle Quay, she loaded a cargo of scrap. Although detained as being unseaworthy, she was towed from the Tyne with permission for a single voyage to a scrapyard and headed for San Esteban de Pravia in northern Spain where demolition was in progress by late December 1980. Sir John Snell, incidentally, had been an electrical engineer and Chairman of the Electricity Commission. He died in 1938.

(Nigel Jones)

The **Lambeth** (1877grt/58) was also built by Hall, Russell at Aberdeen. She was launched on 23 January 1958 and delivered to the South Eastern Gas Board in April of that year. The Board came into existence in 1949, formed by a merger of the South Metropolitan Gas Company and the Wandsworth & District Gas Board. With the merger came a fleet of twelve vessels and the SEGB would eventually build a further nine, all but one of which were "flatirons" for passing beneath the low bridges as they delivered coal to the Board's gas works alongside the Thames. In the late 1960s, natural gas was replacing that generated from coal and, like other ships in the fleet, the **Lambeth** was sold. She was one of four bought by in 1970 by Stephenson Clarke, being renamed **Tarring**. Her new owners traded her more widely but she still worked as a collier though serving more destinations than in her SEGB years. In this photograph, she is about to pass beneath the Severn Bridge on 4 August 1979, heading for Larne with a cargo of cement clinker loaded at Sharpness. After a decade in the Stephenson Clarke fleet, she was sold to Panamanian-flag operators and renamed **Arring**. A further name variation occurred in 1982 when she was renamed **Tarry**. She spent most of 1984 at Glasgow, having arrived there from Kilroot on 11 January. She was eventually sold for demolition and on 5 October 1984 arrived in the Mersey to be scrapped on the foreshore east of Garston.

(Cedric Catt)

The **Yewmount** (1031grt/56) was built by James Lamont & Co Ltd at its Castle Yard in Port Glasgow. She was launched on 20 October 1955 and delivered to Glasgow owner John Stewart & Co Ltd in January 1956. This company always used the Lamont yard for its new vessels. Like many shipyards on the Clyde, it suffered difficulties in the 1970s and the final ship was launched in 1978. In 1974, the **Yewmount** was sold to Mediterranean operators and renamed **Elias G 2**. Four years later she became **Elpis N** and finally **Atlantis I** in 1981. She was scrapped at Perama in 1985. The **Yewmount** was photographed at the West Wharf in Millbay Dock, Plymouth, on 23 August 1972. This berth is now used by Brittany Ferries vessels. Dominating the background is a grain silo built in the 1930s and demolished during the first five months of 2008.

(The late Peter Townsend, Ron Baker collection)

The **Corburn** (2059grt/53) was a product of the Goole Shipbuilding & Repairing Co Ltd. She was launched on 17 January 1953 and delivered in March 1953. She was owned by Wm Cory & Son, a company long associated with the coal trade and whose central funnel marking was an appropriate black diamond. No doubt it would be a cargo of coal that was in her hold as she departed from Swansea on 30 September 1972. By this date she was near the end of her Cory career for she was bought by Greek owners in 1972 and renamed **Aigeorgis**, this becoming simply **Giorgis** in 1976. She did not last out the 1970s. Laid up at Piraeus from 25 July 1978, she left on 15 September 1979, bound for demolition at Brindisi.

(Nigel Jones)

The post-war years saw a huge amount of reconstruction work in Europe. National economies began to recover and trade in raw materials and finished products began to prosper. Shipowners invested in new tonnage, a good example in the UK being the family-owned company of F T Everard. One of its ships built in the mid-1950s, was the **Centurity** (780grt/56), so named because it was thought to be the company's 100th vessel. Launched by Goole Shipbuilding & Repairing Co Ltd on 22 September 1956 and delivered in November 1956, she remained in the Everard fleet until November 1975 when sold to Cypriot-flag operators and renamed **Tempesta**. Her eventual fate is unknown - she was deleted from *Lloyd's Register* in 1987. Apart from fishing vessels, much of the output of the Goole yard during the 1950s was destined for the Everard or Cory fleets. This photograph shows the **Centurity** leaving Par on 23 July 1975.

(The late Peter Townsend, Ron Baker collection)

Built by Clelands (Successors) Ltd at Wallsend on the River Tyne, this coaster was completed in August 1958 and entered the fleet of Coast Lines Ltd as **Somerset Coast**. The following year she was sold to Queenship Navigation Co Ltd and became **Richmond Queen**, a name she retained until 1974 when she was sold to Gomba Shipping Ltd and became **Gomba Enterprise**. Two years later, she was sold and renamed **Atlantic Enterprise**. On 27 October 1977, she arrived at Bremen for repaint which seems to have been a protracted affair. She was still there seven months later and on 20 June 1978, she heeled over at dolphins.

Considered to be beyond economical repair, she was sold for demolition and left Bremen in tow for Brake on 18 July. She was photographed as she left Plymouth's Sutton Harbour on 15 July 1968. Incidentally, in a photograph of her taken at the same location three years later, her funnel bore the word ESK, ownership having transferred to Eskglen Shipping Co. Ltd.

(The later Peter Townsend, World Ship Photo Library)

The Sunderland shipyard of Austin & Pickersgill Ltd will always be associated with the SD14 design of cargo ship but prior to the development of that iconic design, it was an important builder of a wide variety of other ships. The **Greathope** (2646grt/58) was built for the Newbiggin Shipping Company, of Newcastle. She was launched on 28 April 1958 and completed in August of that year. In 1964 she entered the fleet of Shipping & Coal Ltd by whom she was renamed **Queensland** and remained in this fleet until 1976 when she was bought by Greek owners and

renamed **Pambola**. Later changes of identity saw her become **Astarte** in 1981, **Maya** in 1983 and **Gulf Carrier** in 1985. Now flying the flag of Honduras although owned locally in Piraeus, she was photographed at anchor in Piraeus Roads on 2 September 1985. In 1988, she was sold again and renamed **Kalam** and then **Sea Trans I** in 1989. On or about 3 June 1989, she was reported to be aground off the north-west coast of Somalia after suffering engine trouble and being abandoned by her crew.

(Nigel Jones)

The distinctive lines of the **Pauline H** (1093grt/53) suggest a coaster built at a British yard. In fact, she was built at the Troon yard of Ailsa Shipbuilding Co Ltd. She was launched on 14 May 1953 as **Pearl** for Wm Robertson Shipowners Ltd and delivered to this company in September of that year. After 19 years' service, she was sold and renamed **Pauline H**; as such she was photographed outward bound in the New Waterway on 26 May 1975. By this time she had lost her three 3-tonne derricks which served her two hatches, two of these derricks being worked from a midships mast which has also been removed. Later sales saw her renamed **Maymoore** in 1978, then **Arios** and **Simul** in 1980. She arrived at Gadani Beach for demolition on 6 September 1982.

(Nigel Jones)

The *Fenella* (1019grt/51), seen at Douglas on 31 May 1971, was the third ship of this name to serve the Isle of Man Steam Packet Co Ltd. She was built by the Ailsa Shipbuilding Co Ltd at Troon and launched on 6 August 1951. Costing a reported £163,783, she was delivered in December of that year and took up service between Liverpool and Douglas with only very occasional calls at Ramsey. She was notable in being the first motor ship built for the company, being powered by a 7-cylinder British Polar diesel engine. She also offered accommodation for her crew that was far superior to any previous ship in the fleet. In addition to carrying conventional breakbulk cargo, she had demountable pens for up to 100 animals on her main deck. These were always discharged at the Woodside lairage in Birkenhead. When the Steam Packet Company accepted the fact that the future lay in unitised cargoes, the days of the *Fenella* were clearly numbered because the layout of her decks and her cargo gear were unsuited for handling containers and also for conversion. She was sold to Cypriot-flag operators and, named *Vasso M*, left the Mersey on 9 February 1973 having been laid up in Morpeth Dock, Birkenhead, since 27 December 1972. Her end came after she had been severely damaged off Damietta on 2 February 1977.

(Nigel Jones)

With the Isle of Man Steam Packet Co Ltd committed to the development of unit load traffic in 1972, it converted its conventional coaster **Peveril** (1048grt/64) into a cellular container ship for handling such cargoes. To ensure a daily service the Company chartered the **Spaniel** (891grt/55) from the Belfast Steamship Co Ltd, a subsidiary of Coast Lines Ltd, in July 1973. This coaster had been built at the Greenock shipyard of G Brown & Co (Marine) Ltd as **Brentfield** for the Zillah Shipping Co Ltd. She was launched on 21 June 1955 and handed over in October. In November 1958, she returned to her builder for conversion into a container vessel and she was renamed **Spaniel** in early 1959. So successful was she that

the Steam Packet Company bought her in late October 1973 and renamed her **Conister** in December. She was taken to the Ailsa yard in Troon for further modifications to meet the Company's requirements. She eventually became redundant because the Company realised that it would have to invest in roll-on/roll-off facilities. Following the successful installation of a linkspan at Douglas in early June 1981, the **Conister** made her final commercial voyage on 16 June and was sold for demolition near Aviles in Spain in November 1981. We see her heading into the Mersey from Liverpool's Gladstone Lock on 4 April 1975.

(Neil Burns)

The **Hong Leong** (MYS, 867gt/53), photographed at Port Klang on 23 June 1998, has a remarkable history. Like the **Conister**, she was built at the George Brown's Greenock yard and she too had a Coast Lines connection, being delivered to its subsidiary Tyne Tees Steam Shipping Co Ltd as **Netherlands Coast** in June 1953. She spent many years linking Amsterdam and Rotterdam to Newcastle and also delivered occasional cargoes of silver sand to Sunderland. In 1968 she was sold to Israeli operators and, now renamed **Bat Harim**, joined several other former British vessels of a similar size in the fleet of Ofer Brothers (Holdings) Ltd. In 1974, she was briefly renamed **Woodcock** before being sold for service in the Far East as **Hong Leong**. Initially trading under the flag of Panama, she switched to that of Malaysia in the early 1980s and, although changing owners on several occasions since then, she has retained that name.

(Nigel Jones)

The **Brandon** (586grt/57) was very much a Bristol Channel vessel. Her origins were on the English side of the Channel. She was built by Charles Hill & Son at the company's yard in Bristol and was launched on 28 February 1957. She was delivered to Bristol-based Osborn & Wallis on 12 June and was an almost identical sister to the **Colston** built two years previously at the same yard for the same owners. Both ships delivered coal from Newport to Portishead until 1961 when they began to trade more widely, often taking coal to power stations at Yelland and Hayle. Both were sold to W E Dowds Ltd, of Newport, in 1970. Sold on a decade later, they were not renamed; nor were they renamed when sold again as a pair

in 1983 although the buyers did consider changing the name of **Brandon** to **Racebank**. In 1987, the **Brandon** was acquired by Caribbean owners but suffered engine failure when crossing the Atlantic. She was towed back to Lisbon and, after being laid-up there for two years, was sold to local shipbreakers who demolished her during December 1989. We see her here in the Bristol Channel on a sunny but cold 18 November 1981 in the colours of Franco British Chartering Co Ltd.

(Danny Lynch)

The **New Start** (345grt/59) was launched at the Beverley shipyard of Cook, Welton & Gemmell on 14 March 1959 and delivered as **Onward Progress** to Fleetwood Tankers Ltd on 10 June of that same year. She was the second tanker to be acquired by this company which had been established to deliver bunker fuel from the oil refinery at Heysham to trawlers working out of Fleetwood. Her builders were well-known for the construction of trawlers and some aspects of trawler design were evident in the tanker, notably at the stern. In her first year of service, she delivered 78 cargoes from Heysham to Fleetwood but, being chartered by Shell-Mex & BP, she also made 23 voyages to Workington, 13 to Kirkcudbright and occasional visits to ports such as Caernarvon and Barrow. Sold out of the fleet in 1974, she was renamed **New Start** in 1975 and classed for use as a water tanker. A further sale in 1979 saw her become an effluent tanker and we see her at Newport on 28 August of that year. She was bought by Captain Peter Herbert in May 1987 and detained at Bideford one month later. Finally, on 7 July 1987 she left Bideford under tow, bound for demolition at Garston.

(Danny Lynch)

Our final British-built vessel, before moving on to coasters from Dutch yards, is the **Esso Brixham** (758grt/57) which was a product of the Philip & Son shipyard in Dartmouth. She was launched on 10 July 1957 and delivered on 12 November. Despite her name, she was intended to work as a bunkering vessel on the Mersey in addition to coastal duties. She left the Esso fleet in 1979 following a period of lay-up at Marchwood from September 1978 and was purchased by a company connected to Tyne-Tees Waste Disposals Ltd. She was renamed **Brixham** and transferred to the flag of Panama. This proved to be a short-term move for she was scrapped at Middlesbrough between May and October of the following year. Here we see her arriving at Goole on 29 June 1977. She was a fairly regular caller bringing cargoes of bitumen for Knottingley Tar Distillers.

(Neil Burns)

International Shipbrokers Ltd dates back to 1933 when it was founded in the City of London as a shipowning and shipbroking company. It was established by London-based members of the Van der Eb family, of Rotterdam, which had been involved in the operation of coastal vessels since the early years of the 20th century. By the 1950s, some coasters in the fleet were registered under the Dutch flag, others under the British flag. The *John-V* (NLD, 499grt/57) was built at the Firma Gebr. Niestern & Co shipyard in Delfzijl and launched on 28 May 1957.

She completed trials on 4 September and entered service for her owners three days later. The photograph shows her arriving in Barry's No.2 Dock in July 1977. The ship seen in the middle distance is the *Orduna* of the Pacific Steam Navigation Company. The *John-V* was sold to owners based in the Caribbean in early 1988. After a 17-day stay at Mistley, she departed on 21 March 1988, bound for Demerara via Brest. At the time of writing in mid-2008, she remains at work in the Caribbean.

(Peter Olsen)

The next nine pages look at coasters built at yards on the Winschoterdiep, still a busy location for shipbuilding. The **Reine des Anges** (FRA, 499grt/58) was launched on 26 October 1957 at the Scheepswerven Gebr van Diepen shipyard in Waterhuizen at the western end of the Winschoterdiep and opened in 1878. She was delivered to original owner Scheepvaart Mij. Saskia, of Rotterdam, as **Willem Cornelis**. In 1966, she was sold to French owners and was renamed **Reine des Anges**. Under this name, she was one of several French-flagged coasters to trade between ports in south-west England and northern France with cargoes of china

clay. After a decade under the French flag, she was sold for trade in the Mediterranean and hoisted the Greek flag as **Volos II**. The fourth flag of her career came in 1981 when she was bought by Syrian interests and renamed **Ahsan I**, becoming **Mohammad I** four years later. Under this name she continued to trade in the Mediterranean as a container vessel but she still had her original cargo derricks. In 2000, a further sale saw her renamed **Fatimah 1**. Her name was deleted from registers in December 2006. This photograph was taken as she was leaving Plymouth on 17 July 1970.

(Terry Nelder)

It is the central section of the Winschoterdiep which has always been the most productive in shipbuilding terms. The **Aruba** (NLD, 445grt/51) was built at the N.V. Scheepswerf "Voorwaarts" v/h E J Hijlkema shipyard in Martenshoek. Voorwaarts was the name eventually given to the shipyard of E J Hijlkema about which we shall say more on the next page. The **Aruba** was launched on 21 October 1950 and was delivered to J R Bonninga, of Groningen, on 8 March 1951. Unusually, she remained with her original owner throughout her career which ended when she sailed from Drogheda to Dublin for demolition, arriving on 23 February 1974. She is highlighted by the low winter sun as she leaves Barry on 13 December 1969.

(Nigel Jones)

Our front cover photograph depicts the **John Mitchell** built at the Hijlkema shipyard in Martenshoek as yard number 2/65. The **Aurora** (NLD, 381grt/56) was built as the yard's number 2/61. Launched in November 1955, she was delivered early the following year to Groningen owner Harry Frank and placed in Wagenborg management. In August 1978, she transferred to Panamanian registry although no flag is evident as she sails down the Ouse when outward bound from Selby on 24 March 1979. Very much in evidence, though, are the red oxide patches which make a vivid contrast with the bright green paint. In August 1981, she was sold to Spanish owners but retained her Panamanian registry. Following a further sale in 1985, she was renamed **Nabucodonosor** and appeared briefly in movement reports, trading mainly between Spain and Morocco. Her name was removed from *Lloyd's Register* in 1988 because of lack of information. The shipyard was established by Lukas Johannes Hijlkema in the 1930s and initially built tugs. His three sons became involved in the early 1950s and were keen to build coasters. To allow them to build longer vessels, part of the family home had to be demolished. It is worth noting that although literary sources say that the yard was in Martenshoek, builders' plates give the location as Hoogezand. Martenshoek is part of the town of Hoogezand.

(Bernard McCall)

Photographed at Sandfield wharf, Saul, on the Sharpness - Gloucester canal on the evening of 25 October 1981 as she waited to discharge a cargo of cal-mag from Pasajes, the *Emma* (PAN, 499grt/57) is an example of a traditional Dutch coaster with masts and derricks removed and replaced by much lighter structures. Built at the Bodewes Scheepswerven shipyard in Martenshoek, established in 1812, she was launched as *Voorwaarts* on 14 March 1957 and completed on 20 May in that year. After passing through the hands of various Dutch owners, she was acquired in September 1978 by Panamanian-flag operators based in Denmark and renamed *Frederika*. With managers based in Rotterdam, she continued to trade in northern Europe. In 1979, she was bought by Bona Maritime Ltd, a company established at Looe by E A Clayton & Sons but she remained under the flag of Panama and was renamed *Emma* after the daughter of her Master, Captain Mike Clayton. Sold to Caribbean owners in May 1984, she was renamed *Vincentian* and then *Emma A*. In 1989 she became *Endezo* in 1992 and *Lady Kimberley* five years later. On 10 May 1997, she was sunk as an artificial reef at Palm Beach.

(Cedric Catt)

Built at the Gebr Coops shipyard in Hoogezand, the **Majorca** (NLD, 499grt/57) seems to have had a relatively uneventful career. In 1979, she was transferred to the flag of Panama and then to that of the Irish Republic. This photograph shows her arriving at Great Yarmouth on 15 September 1981 almost exactly one year before she met her end on 18 September 1982. On passage from Terneuzen to Teignmouth, her cargo shifted and she sank some twenty miles off Berry Head.

The Coops shipyard opened in the latter half of the 19th century. Facing financial problems in the 1970s like so many other shipyards in northern Europe, it diversified into building parts for ships and supplying these to other yards. Formally established in 1979 and trading as Coops & Nieborg, it has become a very successful supply company.

(Bernard McCall collection)

Almost at the eastern end of the Winschoterdiep is Zuidbroek where Grol's Scheepswerven built many coasters. The company moved to this location from Veendam in 1926 and it continued in business until the late 1960s. The *Plancius* (NLD, 498grt/55) was launched on 3 September 1955 for brothers Jan and Gerrit de Boer, of Delfzijl. Handed over on 10 November, she was placed under Wagenborg management but on 7 December ownership was transferred within the de Boer family and on 26 August 1957, management was switched to Carebeka. On 3 March 1972, she came into British ownership when acquired by D Cumming & Co Ltd by whom she was renamed *Pamela C*. In March of the following year, she was bought by W N Lindsay (Shipowners) Ltd, of Leith, and renamed *Roselyne*. The style of the owning company changed several times over the ensuing years until she was sold to owners in Anguilla in December 1980.

Our photograph shows her discharging grain at the Hudson Ward silos in Goole's South Dock on 20 November 1977. Her delivery voyage to the Caribbean was not without its problems and she was at Tenerife with engine problems in mid-January 1981. In 1985, she was reported to be in the Surinam river with engine problems but she remained listed in *Lloyd's Register* until 2000.

(Bernard McCall)

The **Afife M** (TUR, 471gt/54) was a product of the E J Smit & Zoon shipyard at Westerbroek. She was launched as **Alcetas** on 30 May 1954 and delivered on 20 August to Nieuwe Kustvaart Mij. NV, of Amsterdam, and on charter to KNSM. In 1972 she was sold to Panamanian flag operators and renamed **Etas**. Four years later, a further sale saw her become **Mare 1** and then she was renamed **Sunnybeach** (also rendered in some sources as **Sunny Beach**) in 1979. 1991 saw a sale to Turkish owners by whom she was renamed **Kaptan Yasar Akbas** but her name was later removed from *Lloyd's Register* as her existence was in doubt. She did indeed exist and a further sale within Turkey saw her become

Afife M in 2001. She was photographed as she passed through the Bosphorus on 19 June 2003. After a collision off the coast of Cyprus on 31 October 2004, she was towed to Iskenderun in Turkey and there berthed in the railway harbour where she was arrested. The owner was refused permission to repair his ship and took his case to court. After 70 days, the judge decided in the owner's favour and the ship was allowed to go to a repair yard. In 2006, she was renamed **Kaptan Salih**. She was sold to Syrian owners in April 2007 but without change of name.

(Nigel Jones)

25

In the mid-1960s, several Dutch-built and Dutch-owned coasters were acquired by French owners and were often seen loading china clay in Devon and Cornwall for ports in northern France. The **Le Trieux** (FRA, 499grt/58) was built at the Foxhol yard of N.V. Ferus Smit v/h J Smit & Zoon. Still a prolific builder of coastal vessels, this yard should not be confused with that of E J Smit mentioned in the previous caption. Originally named **Lion**, this coaster came into French ownership in 1965 and became **Le Trieux**. Following sale to eastern Mediterranean operators in 1978, she was renamed **Bejou** and later became **Husni** (1984), **Sky 1** (1987), **Lama** (1990) and **Crescent I** (1993). She is thought to be still in service and flying the flag of Honduras. There appeared to be a storm imminent when she was photographed at Par on 15 July 1973.

(The late Peter Townsend, Ron Baker collection)

The **Hassan** (LBN, 398grt/51) was built by Gebr. Suurmeijer, N.V. "Vooruitgang". She was launched as **Audacia** at this company's yard at Foxhol on 2 August 1951 and underwent trials on 29 September before entering service two days later for original owner C Minnaar, of Overschie. She was sold to Rederij Pinkster, of Voorthuizen, in 1963 and was renamed **Pioneer**, eventually leaving the Dutch flag when sold in 1972 to Lebanese owners by whom she was renamed **Hassan**. She was photographed in Limassol Roads on 26 September 1990. When undergoing repairs at Tripoli on 1 June 1992, there was an explosion on board followed by a fire which caused serious damage. Some reports suggest that she was not sold for scrap until 1998.

(Nigel Jones)

We temporarily move away from the north-eastern area of the Netherlands to Friesland in the north-west where several significant yards have been located. One of these is the C Amels & Zn shipyard in Makkum. In 1955, this yard had asked Amsterdam-based ship architect Peter Lalleman to design a coaster able to carry about 500 tonnes of cargo on a gross tonnage of just under 400 grt. This design proved to be hugely successful and the **Gouweborg** (NLD, 394grt/58) was the third in the series. She was launched on 30 November 1957 and handed over to Wagenborg on 9 January 1958. Four other yards built coasters of the same design as it became popular, especially for Wagenborg which owned or chartered most of these ships. The **Gouweborg** became **Louise** in 1969 and was distinguished by her red hull, an unusual colour in the fleets of Dutch operators. This photograph was taken at Plymouth on 3 August 1972. Sold in 1978, she was renamed **Louise Joan** under the Red Ensign but switched to the flag of the Cayman Islands in 1979. In 1982 a further sale saw her become **Captain Jean**. She remains listed as such in *Lloyd's Register* although, for no apparent reason, her gross tonnage has been listed as 295 since the mid-1980s. The Amels shipyard opened in 1918 but since 1982 has concentrated on the building of luxury yachts.

(The late Peter Townsend, World Ship Photo Library)

When discussing the building of modern coastal vessels, there is often reference to the construction of a ship's hull at one yard and completion at another. This is certainly not a new method of construction, although what is relatively new is the use of yards in eastern Europe for building the hull. The **Mouhsein** (QAT, 399grt/59) is an example of a vessel built in two yards although, this being the 1950s, both yards were in the Netherlands. The hull was built at the Scheepswerf Friesland yard in Lemmer and completion was at the Amels yard in Makkum. Her launch date is given as 15 November 1958 and she was delivered as **Batavier V** to Wm H Müller & Co, of Rotterdam, on 29 January 1959. Her first change of name came in September 1976 when she was sold to Cypriot-flag operators and renamed **Satellite**. Six years later, she was sold to buyers in the Middle East,

based in Doha, but without change of name. In 1985 she was sold to another Doha-based owner and was converted to a livestock carrier. As built, she was 69,77 metres long between perpendiculars. This was reduced to 65,99 metres during the conversion. Her gross tonnage was reduced from 499 to 399. It was presumably during this reconstruction that she lost her cargo gear. Originally she had a bipod mast with four derricks amidships and a goalpost mast with two derricks immediately forward of the bridge. She was deleted from *Lloyd's Register* in 2001 but this photograph shows her in Dubai creek and named **Mouhsein** on 14 March 2003. She was owned in Qatar but flew the flag of North Korea and was subsequently scrapped at Alang in January 2004.

(Roger Hurcombe)

We now look at two coasters built in other parts of the Netherlands. The **Superior Producer** (NLD, 400grt/57) was another coaster to have been constructed at two yards. Her hull was built at the De Rietpol shipyard in Spaarndam, near Haarlem, with completion being undertaken at the Kramer & Booy shipyard in Kootstertille. Delivered in November 1957 and initially named **Andromeda**, she became **Superior Producer** in 1962. She had accommodation for five passengers and, together with fleetmate **Superior Trader** (NLD, 329grt/60), operated a regular service between Scheveningen and Great Yarmouth that had started in the late 1950s. Market produce such as lettuce and tomatoes were brought from the Netherlands, whilst cattle and caravans were taken on the return voyage. There were daily arrivals in Great Yarmouth, except on Saturdays. Two brand new ships

entered service on the route in 1966. Ownership of all four vessels was registered in the name of Norfolk Lijn BV. By the end of the decade, a linkspan had been built and the service became roll-on/roll-off. Ownership of Norfolk Lijn passed to Unilever and then to A P Møller, and the ports served in 2008 are Felixstowe and Vlaardingen. As for the **Superior Producer**, she was sold to Panama-flag operators in 1970 (some sources say 1972) and was renamed **Superior Producer F A** for trade in the Caribbean. Her end came when she foundered shortly after leaving Curaçao on 30 September 1977. Our photograph shows her at Dover on 8 July 1970, possibly loading for her delivery voyage.

(Peter Glenn)

The **Drie Gebrs** (NLD, 496grt/52) was built by Terneuzensche Scheepsbouw Mij. for Lambertus Davids, of Delfzijl, and was operated by the Wagenborg company. Although clearly written as such on the ship, the name (which means "Three Brothers") was always written in full as **Drie Gebroeders** in Lloyd's Register. The coaster transferred to the flag of Panama in 1969 and some sources suggest that her name was written in full from 1974. Our photograph shows her in Weston Point Docks on 16 March 1975, suggesting that although she may have been officially renamed in the previous year, it had not been changed on her bows. In 1983, she was sold to owners in Guyana but again without change of name. She disappears from Lloyd's Register in 1989 and her eventual fate is uncertain.

(Neil Burns)

31

Our review of coasters built in Dutch yards has been largely geographical so far but we temporarily leave this approach to look at a couple of tankers. In the 1950s, Dutch shipyards concentrated on the building of dry cargo coasters; tankers rarely featured. This was rather surprising because the petrochemical industry in the Netherlands was growing rapidly in the post-war years. The *Corrie Broere* (NLD, 500grt/53) was built at the shipyard of de Haan & Oerlemans' Scheepswerf N.V. in Heusden where she was completed as *Corrie B* in February 1953. In 1960, she was renamed *Corrie Broere* and her tank section was renewed in 1962. Coming to the end of her career in Dutch ownership, she is seen leaving Avonmouth on 30 October 1971. She was sold the following year and sailed to the warmer climes of the Mediterranean where she traded as *Elpida III* for Greek owners. Subsequent sales saw her become *Michail* in 1976 and *Megalochari* in 1977. After a life of over half a century, she was sold for demolition in Turkey and arrived at Aliaga on 17 July 2004.

(Nigel Jones)

Our second tanker was not even built for Dutch owners but the shipyard involved takes us conveniently back to the Winschoterdiep. The N.V. Scheepswerf "Waterhuizen" J Pattje shipyard at Waterhuizen, which opened in 1778 and survived until 2001, constructed the *Kyndill* for the Shell company of Iceland. Of 778grt, she was launched on 20 June 1955 and delivered on 17 October. She was one of only two ships built at the yard in 1955 and was significant in being the first tanker to be built there. Indeed, no further tankers were built at this shipyard until 1968. In 1974, she entered the fleet of Effluents Services Ltd, of Macclesfield, and was renamed *Thirlmere*. She is seen leaving Birkenhead at the start of a voyage to the dumping ground in Liverpool Bay on 15 April 1975. She was sold for scrap in summer 1988 and arrived for demolition at Milford Haven on 1 August of that year.

(Neil Burns)

Groningen and its surrounding area was renowned for building coastal vessels, often for local ownership and it is appropriate that we leave Dutch shipyards with two vessels built in the city. The **Result** (NLD, 457grt/53), seen leaving Plymouth's Sutton Harbour on 8 June 1970, was launched at the Groningen shipyard of Noord-Nederlandsche Scheepswerven on 1 August 1953 and completed in late September 1953; some sources give the date of completion as 24 September, others as 30 September. During her career, she passed through the hands of several Dutch owners but was noted flying the flag of Panama at Par in late January 1973. In March 1976 she was acquired by Syrian owners and renamed **Manal**, becoming **Yamameh** in 1984. As such, she arrived at Piraeus on 25 July 1985 and would appear to have been laid up there until 1988 when she was sold for demolition.

(Terry Nelder)

This vessel has proved to be one of the most remarkable survivors in this book. She was one of two sisterships built at the Scheepsbouw Unie shipyard in Groningen and was launched as **Ella** on 5 April 1955, being delivered after successful trials on 25 May. Of distinctive low air draught design, both ships were designed for trading to Paris for the Swedish Götha Line, taking steel, rails and paper on the southbound voyage, along with Husqvarna tractors as deck cargo. For the return journey, the ships used to load Renault and Citroën cars. The round trip would take fourteen days. When built, the **Ella** had a mast and two 3-tonne derricks amidships between the two hatches but these were later removed. Replaced by more modern ships in the mid-1960s, she was sold and renamed **Vlieree** in April 1966 and she was transferred to the flag of Panama in 1973. Our photograph shows her leaving Par on 2 August 1974.

(The late Peter Townsend, Ron Baker collection)

On 21 January 1981, the **Vlieree** arrived at Harlingen from Antwerp and was laid up. In 1982, she moved to the Welgelegen shipyard in Harlingen and was converted from a general cargo ship to a hopper/suction dredger. This extensive conversion involved equipping her with bottom doors. She was also lengthened by 20,4 metres and widened by 2,1 metres, the result of all these modifications being to increase her gross tonnage to 1097gt. She now flies the flag of Honduras. She was photographed at Vlissingen on 20 June 2007.

In 1964, the Unie shipyard and Scheepswerf Gideon v/h J Koster Hzn. joined with the Noord-Nederlandsche Scheepswerven to form Nieuwe Noord-Nederlandsche Scheepswerven but this combined unit succumbed to financial difficulties in 1986.

The Eemskanaal connects Groningen to the sea and meets the estuary of the River Ems at Delfzijl. The Ems forms the border between the Netherlands and Germany and it is to German shipyards that we now turn.

(Martin Wright)

The **Lesrix** (726grt/ 57) was built at the Jos L Meyer shipyard in Papenburg, upstream of Leer on the Ems. She was delivered as **Whitehaven** to the Whitehaven Shipping & Trading Co Ltd in November 1957. Renamed **Lesrix** in 1964 and lengthened in 1971, she proved to be rather problematical and suffered various machinery failures. She did little trade in the latter half of the 1980s. Laid-up at Hull in early May 1985, she was sold a year later, renamed **Nan 1** and placed under the flag of Honduras. In mid-October 1987, she was again laid-up but now at Rochester. When sold for demolition in August 1990, it seemed as though her demise was imminent and she was towed to Bruges for demolition, leaving the Medway on 12 September 1990. She escaped the cutter's torch, however, and was resold for further trade. She re-appeared in movement reports in mid-July 1992 when she sailed from Rotterdam to Kinsale and thence to Boulogne and ultimately into the Mediterranean and the Black Sea port of Bourgas. Early in 1993, she was renamed **Shaman 1** and, now under the Syrian flag, was trading in the eastern Mediterranean with occasional and protracted visits to Constanta. She disappeared from movement reports after arriving in Beirut in December 1993. It was reported that she was renamed **Urouba I** in 1994 and she remained listed under this name in *Lloyd's Register* until 2005. This photograph shows her at Hayle on 16 May 1973.

(Terry Nelder)

The **Miss Nauel** (HND, 361gt/57) was built at the Jadewerft shipyard in Wilhelmshaven as **Johann Schepers** for Kapitän Rudolf Schepers, of Haren/Ems. In July 1959, she was sold to Carl Lehnkering, of Duisburg, and renamed **Carl Lehnkering**. In 1968 she was bought by C E Jagemann, of Stade, and became **Angela Jagemann**. On 21 June 1979, she left Hamburg bound for Panama after sale to Caribbean owners who gave her the name **Mari-Mar M**. Renamed **Miss Nauel** in 1992, she has continued to trade in the area. Our photograph shows her at Colon on 20 March 2002. She appears to have her original mainmast but her foremast has been cut down in size and derricks have been removed.

(David Williams)

Photographed as she berthed at Sharpness on 26 April 1992 at the end of a voyage from Gijon, the *Ingela* (HND, 1483gt/57) was built at the Unterweser shipyard in Bremerhaven. She was launched on 7 October 1957 and completed as *Polchow* the following month. She retained her original name until 1970 when she became *Auguste Schulte* and almost immediately *Irene*. Also in that year, she was lengthened by 9,85 metres at the Jos L Meyer shipyard in Papenburg. In 1978, her name was amended to *Ireen*. In 1983 she was renamed *Westlill* before becoming *Ireen* once again in 1987. It was in 1990 that she was renamed *Ingela*,

a name she retained for five years before becoming *Lavinia* in 1995 following an extensive and costly refurbishment. Latterly owned by Lupin Shipping Ltd, of Varberg, she was used to deliver cargoes of stone from Karlshamn in Sweden to ports in north-eastern Germany until the Autumn of 2005. After a lengthy period laid up at Halmstad, this vessel was sold to Lebanese interests in June 2008 and departed under the name *Tali*, with Lome as her port of registry.

(Nigel Jones)

The **Marco Polo** (DNK, 378grt/56) was also built at the Unterweser shipyard and was launched on 23 May 1956 as **Thebe**. On 10 July, she was delivered to Partenreederei MS "Thebe" with management by the well-known German company Dampfschifffahrts-Gesellschaft "Neptun". She was the first of two sisterships and both entered service on the company's service linking Bremen to Sweden, usually the port of Malmö. In 1967, she was purchased outright by DG Neptun. On 1 April 1971, she left the German flag following purchase by Danish owner T H Hansen, of Thurö, by whom she was renamed **Stevnscarrier**. Sold within Denmark three years later, she was renamed **Marco Polo**. Sold on again in

1980, she was renamed **Fuga**. In early October 1992, she arrived at Rotterdam from Hull and was later arrested for alleged involvement in drug trafficking and laid up. She was confiscated and was sold at auction on 4 June 1995 and, now named **Fuga I**, departed for Curaçao on 20 August. She sank in the Caribbean on 26 July 1996 after encountering heavy weather while on passage from Puerto Cabello to St Maarten with a cargo of bagged cement. Sadly, one member of her crew was lost but six others were rescued by the **Gerina** (NIS, 2130gt/73). Our photograph shows her about to leave Sharpness on the sunny evening of 24 August 1979 after discharging lucerne pellets from Holbæk.

(Cedric Catt)

Remarkably, the **Brake** (ATG, 603gt/57) is still trading in northern Europe as we come towards the end of the first decade of the 21st century. Her present name is appropriate as not only is she registered in Brake but also she was built at the C Lühring shipyard in that port. She was launched on 2 April 1957 and completed on 6 June of that year. Here we see in her later guise at Hull on 10 April 1989 when flying the flag of Antigua & Barbuda. At the time of writing (July 2008), she had transferred to the flag of Tuvalu.

(Roy Cressey)

The **Brake** was originally named **Marlies**, a name she retained until November 1990. During the year preceding her sale, she was a frequent visitor to Aberdeen, making 21 calls to deliver pipes from Rotterdam and Antwerp. This photograph of the **Marlies** was taken at Truro on 15 May 1972. Between 26 November 1961 and 4 August 1975 the **Marlies** brought 63 cargoes of timber from Scandinavia to Truro. Clearly modifications have been made between the dates of the photographs. In March 1978 she went to the shipyard in Elsfleth and was lengthened by 5,6 metres. She returned to the Elsfleth yard in March 1981 for further modifications. As a result of the changes, her gross tonnage figure increased from 423 to 603, and her deadweight changed from 591 to 817.

(Terry Nelder)

The Elsflether Werft shipyard is located on the River Hunte near its confluence with the Weser. The **Natalie** (DEU, 475gt/50) is our first Weselmann coaster but almost unrecognisable from her original appearance. She was launched at Elsfleth on 11 November 1950 and delivered as **Elli Ahrens** to original owner Dietrich Ahrens, of Brake, on 21 December. Two decades later, she was acquired by Hans Schlichting, also of Brake, and renamed **Margot Schlichting**. In 1976, she was fitted with a new engine and in July 1978 she went to the Schlichting-Werft shipyard in Travemünde where she was lengthened by six metres. In 1980, further modifications saw her fitted with aluminium hatchcovers and a bulbous bow. Between 24 February and 17 March 1992, she was at the Detlef Hegemann Rolandwerft shipyard where she was again lengthened by six metres. At the same time, her bulbous bow was removed and fitted on to the **Lilly K** (DEU, 285grt/66). On 25 January 2000, she was sold to Nahmen Christiansen and was renamed **Natalie**. As such she was photographed on the Winschoterdiep on 17 April 2001. Proving that she still had a useful life although 57 years old, she was bought in 2007 by Joachim Janssen, of Timmel, to service a contract requiring the transport of 14,000 tons of stone from Hamburg to the island of Wangerooge where it was needed for strengthening the beach.

(Bernard McCall)

The **Anglesey Trader** (PAN, 376grt/56) was built at the Heinrich Brand shipyard in Oldenburg for Josef Schöning, of Haren/Ems. Initially named **Helena**, she became **Barbara J** following sale to Wilhelm Jüngerhans, also of Haren/Ems, on 16 February 1968. In 1973, she was renamed **Sea Ems** when chartered by Freight-Express Seacon. In 1979 a further sale saw her renamed **Anudo**, the name coming from Udo and Ann, her captain/owner and his wife. Two years later, she was bought by the Carmet Tug Co Ltd. This company was based in Port Penrhyn, near Bangor, in North Wales. This explains her name at the date of the photograph. Sold in 1985 but without change of name, she was laid up on the Thames in June 1985 and sailed for Barranquilla exactly one year later following sale to owners in Colombia. She was renamed **Patricia I** in 1988 and **Fortuna Bay** in 1993. The latter name was modified to **Fortuna Bay I** in 2000. The photograph was taken as she arrived at Barry in September 1981. The tyre fenders on her port side tell us that she was carrying a cargo of explosives transhipped from a larger vessel anchored off the port, the fenders helping to prevent metal-to-metal contact.

(Peter Olsen)

When ships are sold to owners who use an alphabet other than Latin, problems sometimes arise in transliteration. This is often seen in Greek. However, the raised letters of part or the whole of an original name can be immensely helpful as in this example. Clearly seen is the name **Kurt Bastian**, a vessel of 494 gross tons and built at the Heinrich Brand two years before the **Anglesey Trader**. Sold in 1970, she was renamed **Katerina K** and then became **Homer** in 1972. She retained this name for only a year and became **Nicolaos M** in 1973. She is seen here loading at Zakynthos in July 1990. By this date, she had been equipped with an excavator amidships, a common feature on Greek coasters. Her later years became shrouded in mystery. In 1997, she seems to have been "renamed" **Nikolaos M**, though this could have been simply an alternative transliteration. In 2001, *Lloyd's Register* noted that she had been renamed **Sad** under the Belize flag in 1999. Later editions make no mention of this but report her as becoming **Al Murtada** under the Sao Tome flag in 2001. One source noted that she had arrived at Mumbai for demolition on 7 December 2001 whilst another reported she suffered generator damage off the coast of Oman on 9 June 2002. This latter vessel could have been the 1969-built **Al Murtada**.

(Alistair Paterson)

The **Wilma Lucker** (DEU, 384grt/50) was built at the Franz Lürssen Yacht- und Bootswerft shipyard in Bremen-Vegesack. She was launched as **Geversdorf** on 10 July 1950 and delivered in September to her original owner Albert Heitmann, of Geversdorf. Like many other Weselmann coasters, she underwent modifications during her career. In September 1955 she went to the Jadewerft shipyard in Wilhelmshaven and was lengthened by 10,4 metres. This increased her gross tonnage from 299 to 384grt and her deadweight from 425 to 490dwt. In early 1960, she grounded on the Große Vogelsand bank in the Elbe estuary, near the point where Elder Dempster's **Ondo** was to go aground in December of the following year during a valiant but vain attempt to rescue the three-strong crew of the Elbe pilot cutter which had capsized. It was in 1965 that the **Geversdorf** became **Wilma Lucker** after sale to Johann Lucker, of Osten. The next sale saw her remain in Germany, being acquired in 1983 by Hans Christian Nielsen, of Husum, for whom she traded as **Karoline N**. She remained under this name only for three years, arriving in her home port of Hamburg for demolition on 5 May 1986. In superb external condition, she heads up the River Elbe on 3 June 1982.

(Bernard McCall)

The *Jane* (DEU, 421gt/56) is seen at Par on 29 October 1993. She had arrived from Newport (Gwent) and was about to load china clay for Kampen. She was built by Gebr Schürenstedt KG Schiffs- und Bootswerft at its yard at Bardenfleth on the western bank of the Weser, downstream from Bremen. Launched on 5 November 1956, she was delivered to an owner in Elsfleth on 1 December. She would remain in German ownership for a further 39 years, all subsequent owners being based in Elsfleth. When she was lengthened by 9,5 metres in April 1963, it was inevitable that this work would be carried out at the shipyard in Elsfleth. She was eventually sold in Spring 1995 and arrived at Rotterdam from Immingham on 25 May. Destined for work in the Caribbean, she was renamed *Salmon King* and departed for Castries on 9 September. We now move away from shipyards on the Weser to those on northern Germany's other great river, the Elbe.

(Cedric Catt)

The Mützelfeldwerft ship yard in Cuxhaven at the mouth of the River Elbe launched its first ship in 1903 but did not become a productive yard until the 1930s. World War 2 saw the construction of only two tugs at a time when the port of Cuxhaven served as a naval base with a flotilla of the German Mine Sweeping Administration. It was not until 1950 that the yard recommenced production with two Weselmann coasters being built in that year, a third in 1951 and a fourth in 1952. The *Shahin* (PAN, 424grt/52) was the third of the four and was launched as *Hanni-Lene* on 28 November 1951. Delivery to her owner, Georg Behrmann, of Krautsand, was not until 22 November 1952. The Jadewerft shipyard in Wilhelmshaven lengthened several of the Weselmann ships and it was there that

the *Hanni-Lene* was lengthened by 8,7 metres in November 1957. In 1973 she was sold to L E Rohden, of Stade, and was renamed *Collhusen*. Further sales saw her become *Passat II* in 1978 and *Dopas* in 1979 before Alois Beenke, of Hamburg, acquired her in 1981 and renamed her *Shahin*. She was photographed at Par on 26 July 1981, having arrived from Belfast and about to load china clay for Glückstadt. This name lasted for only two years because she was renamed *Ben* in 1983. In 1985 she was purchased by unidentified Greek owners and renamed *Aegeopelagitiki* and she is believed to have been scrapped in Greece in 1990/91.

(Cedric Catt)

After the construction of the four Weselmann ships in the early 1950s, the Mützelfeldtwerft yard produced only one other conventional coaster in the 1950s and we see her in this photograph. The **Lars Bagger** (DIS, 326gt/57) emerged from the yard in 1956 as **Welf** for German owner Friedrich Steffens, of Himmelspforten. In August 1973, she was sold to Danish owners and renamed **Ulsnæs**, becoming **Lars Bagger** after sale to Villy Bagger Jensen in 1989. The yard continues to build ships but has built only one further dry cargo coaster since the one in this photograph and that was in 1985. The **Lars Bagger** is seen here heading eastwards in the Kiel Canal shortly after discharging a cargo at the Kiel grain terminal on 11 January 2001. In May 2008, the coaster was sold because of her owner's ill health and in August 2008, she was renamed **Volo**.

(Oliver Sesemann)

Stader Schiffswerft in Stade was never the most prolific of shipyards, being able to complete three or four coasters annually in the years after World War 2 and the **Llanishen** (VCT, 423grt/55) was the first of four ships completed at the Stade shipyard in 1955. She was built for German owners as **Hermann Elsen** and was sold to other German owners in 1967 when she became **Unitas H**. In 1975, she hoisted the Red Ensign when she was renamed **Nethergate**, becoming **Mortic** in 1976, **Christina Maria** in 1979, **Celtic Clipper** in 1984 and finally **Llanishen** in 1987 when she was owned by Avonmouth-based Runwave Ltd and flew the flag of St Vincent & the Grenadines. This latter part of her career was not without its problems. She was laid up in Barry between 30 March and 16 June 1988. Only twelve days later she arrived at Northwich and remained there under repair until 7 September. It appeared that her troubles were over in 1989. She even took a cargo of explosives to the Mediterranean in June. The optimism was shortlived; she suffered an engine room fire off the Isle of Wight on 12 August 1989 and was towed to Southampton. Repairs would have been too expensive so she was towed to Milford Haven for demolition, arriving on 26 September 1989. This photograph shows her at Sharpness on 28 October 1987. She had been in drydock since arriving from Ramsgate on 28 September and, newly-painted, she was loading 600 tonnes of beans for Bremerhaven.

(Cedric Catt)

The **Chiemsee** (CYP, 488grt/58) was built at Stader Schiffswerft as **Sleipner I** and was lengthened in 1961. In 1969 she was sold and renamed **Edith Holst** and became **Chiemsee** in 1974. Later changes of name saw her become **Amsel** in 1980 and then **Paraguay Ranger** in 1982. As her name suggests, she sailed to South America and was linking ports such as Paranagua and Asuncion by mid-August 1982 although she had been noted at Goole in mid-June. Her stay in South America proved to be surprisingly brief. By the end of the year, she was back in north-west Europe and left Rotterdam for Glasson Dock on 30 December. She had to put in to Plymouth with engine problems. Ongoing problems saw her towed from Cardiff to Rotterdam on 16 March and from there to an unidentified Dutch port in mid-April. Despite these problems, she was deemed worthy of repair although nothing was heard about her until she was reported to have been sold and renamed **Treasure** in 1985. In late July 1985, she was noted at Husum in northern Germany, yet again under repair. She seems to have traded reasonably successfully between the UK and ports in northern Europe until she was laid up at Esbjerg on 1 January 1988. She was later sold for demolition in Denmark. The photograph shows her arriving at Barry in November 1977. Like the **Anglesey Trader** on page 42, she was involved in the transhipment of explosives.

(Peter Olsen)

There is not a cloud in the sky as the **Louise Schupp** (DEU, 949grt/57) approaches Barry on 4 January 1970. This coaster was launched at the Köser & Meyer shipyard in Hamburg on 18 May 1957 and delivered to owner Hamburg-based owner J H T Schupp on 17 July. She came under the Dutch flag in 1971 when bought by owners based in Groningen and was renamed **Marbo**. In the following year, she was renamed **Sylvia V** and transferred to the flag of Panama.

1972 saw her sold to Cypriot-flag owners by whom she was renamed **Darius**, becoming **Palm Wind** two years later. It was reported that she was demolished in 1979 but no further details are known. The Köser & Meyer yard was established as Norderwerft in 1906, becoming Norderwerft Köser & Meyer thirty years later. On 2 January 1973, the yard was taken over by J J Sietas and we shall return to Sietas shortly.

(Nigel Jones)

The **Ostara** (DEU, 422grt/57) was built by W Holst at Cranz-Neuenfelde on the outskirts of Hamburg. She was initially named **Jürgen Stahmer** for Kapitän Franz Stahmer, of Hamburg, and became **Ostara** when bought by Harry Corleis, also of Hamburg, in 1965. She remained in his ownership for twenty years. Sold to other German owners in 1985, she transferred to the flag of Honduras and was renamed **Compass I**. On 1 December 1986, she stranded on the island of Texel after suffering machinery failure when on passage from Colchester to Hamburg. She was broken up in situ. She makes a fine sight as she passes beneath the Humber Bridge on 27 April 1984.

(Bernard McCall)

Before looking at coasters built at other yards on or near the River Elbe, we move briefly to builders on the Baltic coast of Germany. The **Austvik** (NOR, 975grt/57), seen leaving Cardiff on 20 May 1973, was built at the Alfred Hagelstein shipyard in Lübeck where she was launched as **Maria Althoff** on 9 November 1957. It was almost a decade later, in April 1967, that she was bought by Norwegian owners Lorenz Storesund & Sønner, of Torvestad, and renamed **Austvik**. In November 1979, she was sold within Norway to Kaspar Nilsen, of Sand, and she was renamed **Ramsli** in May of the following year. Between November 1984 and July 1988, she lay at the now-defunct Karmsund Verft shipyard, south of Haugesund. She was then acquired by owners based in Dominica and left the shipyard in August, calling at Brest on her way to the Caribbean. There she continued to trade actively, still named **Ramsli**, until she disappeared from movement reports in August 1992. Her last reported sailing was from the Colombian port of Mamonal to nearby Tolu on 22 January 1992.

(Nigel Jones)

The **Hela** (DNK, 348grt/52) was built at the Lübeck shipyard of Orenstein, Koppel & Lübecker. She was launched as **Cambria** but seems to have entered service under the name **Stellaria**. In 1962, she was sold and renamed **Salome**, and became **Hela** in 1966. We see her here at Llanthony Quay in Gloucester Docks on 10 January 1981 after arrival from Sønderborg with a cargo of machinery. This book has several photographs of one ship under two different names, but this is our only example of the same ship featuring twice under the same name. The reason for this is to illustrate a significant modification.

(Cedric Catt)

The **Hela** was one of four small coasters fitted with a bulbous bow at Ærøskøbing in Denmark and this is a prominent feature as she lay at her berth in Århus on 4 August 1992. Her ultimate end was an unhappy one. In November 1993, she was sold to an owner in The Gambia and immediately came under suspicion by the Danish police who started to monitor her movements because of her possible involvement in drugs trade. On 5 January 1994, she left Antwerp on a voyage that took her to Lome, Sao Tome and Morocco. On her return she was intercepted by police near Fåborg on the island of Fyn. The ship was taken to Copenhagen and remained abandoned there for a decade. Following the death of her owner, the ship was sold for demolition at Frederikshavn.

(Bernard McCall)

The **Anglezarke** (608grt/56) was built at the Schlichting Werft shipyard in Travemünde for Hamburg-based tanker owner A F Harmsdorff. She was launched on 15 September 1956 and delivered as **Nessand** on 5 November. In December 1963, she returned to the Schlichting yard to have her original 6-cylinder MAN engine replaced by a 6-cylinder Deutz engine. Following sale in 1967 to German associates of the Danish company Terkol Rederierne, she was renamed **Otto** and this was amended to **Otto Terkol** the following year. On 31 August 1970, she suffered an explosion while discharging gas oil at Rønne on the island of Bornholm. She was towed to Århus and then Fredericia for repair. In the early 1970s, the Terkol company was in dispute with the Danish seamen's union and so flagged out its tankers to Liberia with ownership transferred to satellite companies. Thus the **Otto Terkol** became **Mabuli**. In 1975, she was acquired by Effluents Services Ltd, of Macclesfield, and renamed **Anglezarke**; this company named its tankers after reservoirs in the north of England. Our photograph shows her leaving Goole on 23 September 1977. She was sold for demolition at Garston where she was scrapped in July 1988.

(Neil Burns)

We now begin to move back towards shipyards near the River Elbe and Hamburg. The **Laboe** (DEU, 386gt/54) was built at the Nobiskrug shipyard in Rendsburg, on the northern bank of the Kiel Canal. She was launched on 9 November 1954 and delivered on 13 December as **Magdalene** to Kapitän Hans Peterson, of Elsdorf. Like many coasters of her generation, she was lengthened early in her career, a section 7,9 metres long being added in 1956. Five years later she became **Marianne C** following purchase by Max Claussen, of Flensburg. A further five years elapsed before there was another change of identity which saw her become **Laboe** in the ownership of Gerriet Behrens. On 17 July 1973, while on passage from Finland to Glückstadt, she grounded on a rock off the Swedish coast and suffered serious damage. There was a repair bill of DM110,000 (about £45,000) and a further DM100,000 had to be paid to cover the rescue operation. In 1979, she was acquired by Panamanian-flag interests and renamed **Elst III**. She ceased commercial trade in 1993 and was converted into a floating ice factory at Den Oever by the Afsluitdijk in the Netherlands. This photograph shows the **Laboe** at Sharpness on 13 August 1978. She had brought a cargo of feed pellets from Groningen and sailed to Par two days later.

(Cedric Catt)

The **Ashausen** (DEU, 499grt/58) was built by Kremer Sohn at Elmshorn on the River Krückau north of Hamburg. This yard began production in 1833 and, facing bankruptcy, closed in 1978. This coaster was originally named **Götaland**; she became **Walter Kay** in 1968 and then **Fischland** in 1971. When so named, she almost met her end. On 3 January 1976, she was driven aground by hurricane-force winds in the Weser estuary. Her recovery took three weeks and proved to be a costly operation. She did, however, return to service. All three owners thus far had been based in Hamburg and in 1980, she was bought by Bernhard Matthies, again of Hamburg, and it was then that she was given the name **Ashausen**. Four years later, she left German ownership and headed for the Middle East when bought by owners based in Sharjah and incongruously named the Greenland Shipping Company. She was renamed **Shaheen**, becoming **Al Mamoon** in 1989 and **Amafhh One** in 1990. Her name disappears from Lloyd's Register in 2002. The photograph shows her outward bound from Barry fully laden in May 1981.

(Peter Olsen)

The last three decades of the 20th century proved to be very difficult years for the shipbuilding industry in north-west Europe. Industrial historians and economists can present many reasons for this decline. The yards that did survive and even flourish often did so because they found a niche market or developed standard classes of ships that met imminent and future needs. The Hugo Peters shipyard in Wewelsfleth proved to be one of the survivors, although even that yard almost succumbed early in the 21st century. The *Marie Both* (DEU, 499grt/57), seen at Par on 10 June 1967, was built before such issues were to arise. She was launched on 28 May 1957 for Reederei Both & Co, of nearby Glückstadt. There was a major incident in her career when she sank off Szczecin on 10 August 1968 following a collison with the *San* (see page 72). She was raised on 21 August and repaired.

(The late Peter Townsend, Ron Baker collection)

The *Marie Both* left northern Europe in 1986 following sale to owners in Syria by whom she was renamed *Nouri*. A further sale within Syria saw her renamed *Ramzah 2* (listed as *Ramza 2* in Lloyd's Register) in 1993 and she appeared to be in fine external condition when photographed at Alexandria on 25 June 1993. In 1996, she was renamed *Farah* but this name was short-lived. When berthed at Constanta, she took on a heavy list after loading had been completed on 13 May in that year. She then heeled over and sank alongside the quay. The wreck was removed after the hull had been cut into two sections. The two photographs enable observation of the changes that had been made during the intervening 26 years.

(Nigel Jones)

There can be little doubt that one of the most famous shipyards in northern Europe, and possibly even further afield, is that of J J Sietas which is located at Neuenfelde on the outskirts of Hamburg. We have deliberately left this yard to the end of the section depicting coasters built in Germany. The **Estebrügge** (DEU, 499grt/58), photographed at Par on 8 December 1973, was a product of the Sietas yard and launched on 29 December 1957. The yard was to become well-known for its standard designs but this vessel was delivered before any design identities were being used. She was sold to Greek owners in 1975 and renamed **Toroneos**,

later becoming **Agioi Anargyroi** in 1984 and **Grigoris M** in 1985. She continued to work around the Greek islands for the next decade, the only modification being a grab crane fitted amidships to replace the mast and two 3-tonne derricks. Other coasters from the Sietas yard had all gear later removed although it was common to retain the distinctive goalpost mast. The **Grigoris M** no longer appeared in Lloyd's Register after 2002 so she is thought to have been scrapped.

(The late Peter Townsend, World Ship Photo Library)

The **Ilse Wolter** (DEU, 422grt/55) was an earlier product of the J J Sietas shipyard, a yard whose skilful team of designers has always succeeded in anticipating the needs of owners and operators. This coaster was built as **Nordkap** and was lengthened in 1957. Many other coasters built at the Sietas yard were to be lengthened during their careers. The **Nordkap** was sold and renamed **Ilse Wolter** in 1962. In 1982, she was renamed **Jupiter A** under the flag of Panama and departed for South America to begin a new life trading extensively from Chile as far north as El Salvador. She grounded on Punta Remedios on 7 May 1983 after leaving Acajutla in El Salvador at the start of a voyage to Agua Dulce in Panama and was abandoned after the crew had left the vessel. This photograph was taken at Charlestown on 1 August 1974. We cannot ignore coasters built in the former East Germany where construction proved to be problematic. It is to these that we now turn.

(The late Peter Townsend, Ron Baker collection)

59

When allocating a year to a ship, it is customary to give the year of delivery. In the case of the next two ships, however, registers give them the year of launch. This suits our purposes for they were launched in the 1950s but not delivered until the next decade. The *Aldebaran* (GDR, 617grt/58) was built at the VEB Peene-Werft shipyard in Wolgast. She was one of the Type 840 design, the name coming from the deadweight tonnage of ships in this class. The design was as distinctive as, in the eyes of the author, it was aesthetically pleasing. The ships had a single hold and two hatches served by two 3-tonne cranes. They were built for a crew of eighteen and had one passenger cabin; one is tempted to say that this would be for a government "observer". The first 14 ships in the class were named after stars or constellations in the northern hemisphere. Although launched on 24 July 1958 the *Aldebaran* was not delivered until 19 April 1961. The long delay was caused by the problems experienced in obtaining equipment. She served in the state-controlled fleet of East Germany (more accurately called the Democratic Republic of Germany) for a decade and, after being taken out of service on 24 January 1977, she was sold to Lebanese operators and renamed *Eurabia Bay*. Further sales saw her become *Athlos II* (1978), *Stavros V* (1982), *Aldebaran* and then *Tai Pan* (1989), *Taipan* (1992) and *Pearl* (1993). She remains listed in *Lloyd's Register*, apparently owned by Dubai-based interests. This photograph was taken as she left Plymouth on 15 September 1971.

(Terry Nelder)

The **Poel** (GDR, 617grt/59) was a sistership of the **Aldebaran** but was to have a very different career. She was launched on 12 May 1959 but not delivered until 9 December 1961. The later ships in the series were named after places in the three northern districts of East Germany. In 1964, she was taken to a Dutch shipyard for modifications to enable her to trade in tropical waters. Based in Tema, she then worked on the coast of West Africa for Uniafrica Poland serving as a feeder ship to and from larger vessels and calling at small ports. By the mid-1970s she had returned to northern Europe but was to resume her travels. Records suggest that she was taken out of service on 19 February 1979 and, in a show of solidarity with another Communist government, was transferred to the ownership of the Government of the Socialist Republic of Vietnam. She was renamed **Song Ba** and transferred to the flag of that country. However, she was certainly in the Far East in 1978 and was noted sailing from Hong Kong to Haiphong in September of that year. It is uncertain if she remains in service. This photograph shows her at Par on 20 April 1974.

(The late Peter Townsend, World Ship Photo Library)

We now look at some coasters built in Denmark where the early 1950s saw the development of a design known as "Caroliner". This series was based on that of the **Gertrud Kathrine**, designed in Denmark but built by D E Scarr Ltd at Howden and delivered to Danish owner Carl Georg Christensen, of Sæby, in March 1950. The **Caroline S** (DNK, 159gt/59) was built at Marstal by H C Christensens Staalskibsværft as **Janto** and delivered to Preben Gramstrup Christensen on 21 December 1959. In 1965, Christensen and Albert Petersen exchanged ships, with the latter taking over the **Janto** which he renamed **Jane**. The captain, Gunnar Hansen, took an increasing financial share in the ship until he became sole owner in 1987. The coaster was sold in August 1994 to Foreningen Caroline Samsø and renamed **Caroline Samsø**. Taken over by Foreningen Caroline S on 15 December 2001, she was renamed **Caroline S**. She is now a museum ship used for exhibitions but still carries cargo when required. Our photograph shows her at Horsens on 23 July 2003 as she passes another veteran, **Betty Nordgas**, details of which will be given on page 64.

(Bent Mikkelsen)

Including the **Gertrud Kathrine**, 24 Caroliners were constructed. Two others were built in Svendborg and one in Kørsør but all the remaining ships were built at the H C Christensens yard. The **Jens Wal** (DNK, 199grt/52), photographed arriving at Par on 24 April 1975, was another Caroliner built by H C Christensens. She was one of 17 Caroliners to be lengthened, in her case the work being done at Aabenraa in June 1965. In 1978, she was acquired by owner/master Nils-Henrik Thordsen and renamed **Birgit Thor**. In October of that year, she sank in the Kattegat while on passage from Vejle to Frederiksværk. She had been so overloaded that the hatch could not be closed and during the night the ship filled with water and quickly sank. Tragically three members of her crew were lost but her captain/owner survived. Oddly the ship was not deleted from the Danish register until June 1992 and so the mortgage lasted until this date. With the underwriters refusing to pay for the loss, the ship's owner was financially ruined but escaped prosecution for the deaths of the crewmen.

(The late Peter Townsend, Ron Baker collection)

The Danish port of Marstal has been an important maritime town since it was founded 500 years ago. The shipyard of H C Christensen was one of the town's leading shipbuilders and constructed many fine coasters in addition to the Caroliners. The **Fenja** (DNK, 460grt/53) began life as **Gert Stærke.** She was lengthened in 1961. Sold by owner R Stærke Kristensen after two decades in service, she was bought by Bjorn Erik Bramming, of Frederikshavn, and renamed **Astrid Bramming**. In 1986, she was sold to a Honduras-flag subsidiary and renamed **Fenja**. Following the bankruptcy of the owner in 1988, the ship was abandoned at Frederikshavn but was sold in late 1989 to a company which planned to rebuild her as a tanker. She sailed to the Morsø Værft shipyard at Nykøbing, Mors, but no payment for the conversion was forthcoming and the ship was eventually sold for scrap. The legal complexities surrounding this demolition caused it to be a protracted business and the ship was not deleted from registers until July 1996. Our photograph shows her arriving at Macduff with 639 tonnes of lime on 23 March 1987.

(Alistair Paterson)

The **Betty Nordgas** (DNK, 204gt/58) was the last of four Danish liquefied petroleum gas tankers, all sisterships built by Svendborg Skibsværft. She was built for Nordisk Flaskegas and was launched on 5 September 1958. Within five years, Nordisk Flaskegas had been taken over by Gulf Oil which built a large refinery at Stignæs, near Skelskør and the **Betty Nordgas** transported 90-tonne cargoes of lpg to depots at Helsingborg, Svendborg, Løgstør, Nexø, Odense and also to Oslo Fjord. In May 1985, she was taken over by Kuwait Petroleum following its purchase of Gulf Oil and BP in Denmark. Taken out of commercial service in late May 1991 after the delivery of her final cargo (82.5 tonnes of lpg from Stignæs to Odense), she was eventually bought for use as a houseboat by Danish shipping journalist Bent Mikkelsen. Berthed initially at Århus, she later moved to Horsens. In October 2006, she was bought by a Dutch owner who planned to continue to use the ship as a houseboat but also as a workshop for his trade as a ship's carpenter and repairer.

(Bent Mikkelsen)

The **Tres-Uno** (NOR, 453gt/58) is a coaster of rather unassuming appearance which belies her considerable historical significance. She was built by Alssund Skibsværft at Sønderborg and delivered in August 1958 to Paal Wilson & Co AS, of Bergen. Named **Kanutta**, she inaugurated Wilson's Norge-Rhin Linje (Norway-Rhine Line) and was thus the precursor of the many coasters of familiar light-blue hull that would appear in later years and of a trade which formed the bedrock of the hugely-successful Wilson group in recent years. Since launching that service, she has passed through the hands of several Norwegian owners, one of whom renamed her **Stålvard** in 1966. In May 1987, she was rebuilt as a shelterdecker and in 1992 was fitted with a "new" engine. More correctly, this should be a replacement engine for the 470bhp Kelvin diesel in fact dated from 1978. Further

sales saw her become **Ringhav** (1993), **Vanko** (1994), **Elisabeth** (also 1994), **Ann Elisabeth** (1995) and **Tres-Uno** (1996). It was in May 1996 that she was fitted out as a self-discharge ship. She is seen here on 10 August 1998 between Fredrikstad and Sarpsborg on the Glomma river, the longest river in Scandinavia. Later in 1998, she was sold and renamed **Lise Maleen**. Her varied life continued with more investment. Another new engine was fitted in 1999, this being a Caterpillar diesel of 670bhp and she had further rebuilding in 2000. There were further changes of identity, too, for she became **Stålvard** in 2002, **Bulkmar** in 2003 and **Euro Bulk** in 2004. In August 2007, she reverted to her original name of **Kanutta** and, now flying the flag of Panama, remains in service on the coast of Norway, thus leading us to some vessels built in that country.

(Dominic McCall)

The **Rafiki III** (PAN, 448gt/58) has a more complex history than her appearance would suggest. She was built at Mandal in Norway by Westermoen Båtbyggeri & Mek Verksted and delivered to her initial Oslo-based owner in August 1958 as **Ava**. In 1965, she was adapted to carry cement in bulk and bagged form but converted back to a conventional coaster following sale to an owner in Haugesund in April 1973. Sold on in May 1974, she was converted yet again this time for work in the sand and aggregate trade. Her surgery was not yet over because in February 1986 she was rebuilt as a shelterdecker. Her deadweight was now 750dwt compared to 500dwt when she entered service almost three decades previously. Through all these changes, and changes of ownership not listed here, she retained her original name. She remained **Ava** until a sale within Norway saw her become **Snofjell** in 1998. She took the name **Rafiki III** and switched to the flag of Panama when sold to a certain Emmanuel Mayaka Owanga in 2001. She was photographed at Valletta on 19 October 2001.

(Fred Kissack)

Dry-cargo coasters built in Norway have always had a distinctive appearance, one of the characteristics being the tall tripod foremast as displayed by the **Anders** (NOR, 369gt/57). She was built by Løland Motorverkstad at Leirvik and was delivered to her original Ålesund-based owners as a coaster of 270grt/340dwt in December 1957. Sold in February 1964, she was lengthened ten months later at the Haugesunds Mek Verksted shipyard. Now 16.2 feet (4,94 metres) longer, her gross tonnage increased to 299grt and her deadweight to 450dwt. More surgery was to come when she was modified at Rognan in April 1990 and again her tonnages increased so that she now had a gross tonnage of 369gt and deadweight of 687dwt. Even then, the investment did not end because her original Alpha diesel engine of 420bhp was replaced by a 690bhp Mitsubishi engine in 1992. In this photograph, she is seen sailing from the Kvernhusvik shipyard at Hitra on 30 April 1993. After more than half a century, she remains at work under her original name.

(Geir Ole Søreng)

The **Anavissos II** (GRC, 568grt/58) was one of two sisterships built for Norsk Brændselolje AS, of Svolvær, a Norwegian subsidiary of BP, at the Glommens Mek Verksted shipyard in Fredrikstad. This shipyard was opened in 1898 and built 199 ships until its closure in 1982. Originally named **BP 27**, she and her sistership **BP 28** were built as tankers of 499grt with a deadweight of 740dwt. They were lengthened in 1971 by 72 feet (21,9 metres) and their tonnages changed to 568grt and 905dwt. In 1978, she was acquired by Anavissos Sea Transport Co Ltd and was renamed **Anavissos II** under the Greek flag. Now registered in Laurium, she did not work in the Mediterranean as might be expected but rather in the Bristol Channel where she was used as an effluent tanker working out of Newport. This photograph of her, taken in the Bristol Channel on 1 June 1980, provides clear visual evidence that she had been lengthened. In 1985, she was sold for demolition at Barry where she arrived in October of that year. Demolition proved to be protracted and was not completed until late 1986.

(Danny Lynch)

We now move to coasters built in Sweden. Arriving at Gothenburg and pursued by two gulls on 29 July 2004, the **Framvik** (SWE, 253grt/54) has a fascinating background. She was the second ship to have been built at Oskar Jonsonss Torrdocka, a small shipyard at Kållandsö on Lake Vänern. The original yard, opened in 1945, was built by Oskar Jonsson and his sons, Harry and Valter. The first vessels were made from wood but in 1950 steel from a scrapped vessel was used in the construction of the **Trellevik**, 198grt. The second newbuilding was the all-steel motor tanker **Trellefjord**, 217grt and 280dwt, delivered in 1954 and ultimately to become the **Framvik** seen here. In 1962, this vessel was renamed **Tankö**, then **Trellevik** in 1977 and she became **Framvik** in 1991. Prior to this,

in 1971, she had been lengthened by 6 metres at the shipyard in Karlstad, her tonnages then changing to 253grt and 406dwt. *Lloyd's Register* identifies the building yard as "Bröderna Jonssons Torrdocka, Lidköping". This is doubly incorrect as the yard was not given that name until 1960 when Oskar Jonsson handed it over to his sons, and it is not in Lidköping. In 1987, the yard came into the ownership of Valter Jonsson's sons, Per and Samuel who were joined by their brother Tomas in 1990 when the yard became Kållandsö Varv AB. Still successful, it has built fishing vessels and small ferries since its early focus on the construction of tankers.

(Bernard McCall)

Photographed in sultry lighting at Valletta during July 1979 and flying the Italian flag, one could be forgiven for thinking that the *Verona* (ITA, 499grt/58) was essentially a Mediterranean vessel but the start of her life was very much Scandinavian. She was built by AB Lindingöverken at Lindingö near Stockholm. Launched for Oslo-based owners on 14 December 1957, she was completed in May 1958. Soon after delivery, she was laid up because of poor market conditions.

In January 1960 she was sold within Norway and renamed *Werona*. A decade later, she left Scandinavia following purchase by owners in Naples and was renamed *Verona*. There were two further sales within that Italian city, both without change of name, before she sank on 5 February 1981 just two miles off Cape Bon whilst on passage from Tunis to Sfax.

(Alistair Paterson)

The shipyard at Sölvesborg opened in 1918 and produced a steady stream of ships until the beginning of World War 2. Wartime orders for ships destined for German companies were cancelled by the Swedish authorities but production recovered in the 1950s when the yard concentrated on ships built for customer needs. But financial difficulties were never far away and the yard passed through the hands of various owners during the 1960s and 1970s. When in the ownership of Cityvarvet AB, of Gothenburg, construction of new ships ended in 1981 although minor repairs continued for a further five years. The *Askja* (ISL, 500grt/57) was built by Sölvesborgs Varv for owners in Iceland and was one of several "paragraph" ships constructed in the 1950s, an uncharacteristic early attempt at series building. Still with the same owners, she was renamed *Kljafoss* in 1976. Our photograph depicts her at Weston Point Docks on 20 April 1976.

(Neil Burns)

In 1980, the *Kljafoss* was sold to buyers in the Middle East, becoming *Khalil II* under the Lebanese flag. *Lloyd's Register* notes her conversion from general cargo ship to livestock carrier in 1983 but it may have been carried out before then. She passed through the hands of various owners and was renamed *Tweit II* in 1988, still under the Lebanese flag. Photographed as she passed through the Suez Canal on 23 June 1995, she is still listed in current registers but without details of owner or flag.

(Nigel Jones)

On the next four pages, we look at some coasters built in Poland. The **San** (POL, 487grt/51) was the second in the B51 series of coasters built during the 1950s. Totalling eleven vessels, the first five were built at the Stocznia Gdanska shipyard although the final two of the five were fitted out by Stocznia Gdyndska. The design was a pre-World War 2 design by Ansaldo, of Genoa; hence the well-balanced profile of a classic coaster. All of the first five sported a raked funnel and wooden wheelhouse. Owned by Polska Zegluga Morska, the **San** was sold in September 1974 to the Bangladesh Inland Water Transport Corporation, of Chittagong, and renamed **C 1067**. In 1976, she became **C5-208** but her name was amended the following year to **C5-209** and this may possibly reflect an error in the initial report to *Lloyd's Register*. About 1993, she seems to have reverted to **C 1067** prior to demolition by Bangladeshi breakers. We see her at Par on 11 July 1971.

(Terry Nelder)

The initial five B51 coasters were built between 1951 and 1953. The B51a series comprised the final six vessels which were built in 1958/59. The **Ner** (POL, 474grt/59) was also built by Stocznia Gdanska and was launched on 21 June 1958 but delivery to owners Polska Zegluga Morska did not take place until early the following year. Like so many vessels built for communist countries in the 1950s and 1960s, she had an abundance of accommodation; in her case she could accommodate for 18 crew and 2 passengers. Here we see the **Ner** at Endeavour Wharf, Whitby, on 31 July 1983. In the mid-1980s, she and some of her sisterships were regular visitors to Whitby and other ports in north-east England bringing general cargo from China that had been transhipped in Hamburg. She continued to make these calls after she had been transferred to Honduran-flag ownership in mid-May 1984. On 17 November 1984 she arrived at Pasajes where she was later laid up and was eventually sold to local breakers for demolition which began on 2 January 1986.

(Bernard McCall)

The B53 series of coasters, built for the Polish Steamship Company by Stocznia Imienia Komuny Pariskiej, Gdynia, was numerically larger than the B51 series, and the individual vessels were also larger. There were 35 ships in the series of which 12 were built for Polish ownership although 7 were transferred en bloc to Chinese ownership after only a few months in service. To say that this design was aesthetically flawed would be to give it scant praise! The two-deck accommodation block located three-quarters aft, the tiny funnel perched on top of this, the bare after section containing only a lifeboat on each side - all combined to make this a very unattractive design. The **Jastarnia** (POL, 610grt/55), an example of the B53 design, remained in Polish ownership until mid-September 1976 when she was acquired by Greek-flag owners based in Piraeus and was renamed **Annoula**. Sold on within Greece in 1982, she became **Spyros K** and served for a further three years before being sold to shipbreakers in February 1985, demolition being undertaken at Miligropoulos Shipyards in Perama. She was photographed at Par on 24 October 1973.

(Terry Nelder)

The **Goplana** (POL, 499grt/59) was built at the same yard in Gdynia as the **Jastarnia**. She was the first example of the B57 series, construction of which continued into the 1960s. There were twelve ships in the series, four of the later ones being converted to container ships as we shall see in *Coasters of the 1960s*. The **Goplana** was launched on 15 April 1959 for Polska Zegluga Morska. She had a single bipod mast amidships and four 3-tonne derricks. Later ships were gearless and there were other design modifications. In 1970, ownership was transferred to Polskie Linie Oceaniczne and then in 1976 to Polska Zegluga Baltycka, the latter change seeing her port of registry altered from Szczecin to Kolobrzeg. By the date of this photograph, 4 May 1987, she retained her bipod mast but the derricks had been removed. In excellent external condition, she is seen at Fowey after arrival from King's Lynn and would load china clay for Gdynia. In early December 1989 she was sold to unspecified owners and switched briefly to the flag of St Vincent & the Grenadines with name abbreviated to **Goplan**. On 29 January 1990, she arrived at Gadani Beach for demolition by Pakistani breakers.

(Cedric Catt)

On this page we look at two vessels built in Spain. Throughout the 1970s and 1980s, the busy port of Fowey saw a steady flow of Spanish vessels loading china clay for Mediterranean ports. The ships were often quite old examples in the Spanish merchant fleet but the **Navacerrada** (ESP, 971grt/59) was an exception when photographed loading at Fowey's No. 4 jetty on 30 September 1972 when a mere 13 years old. She was built by Cia Euskaldena at Bilbao and delivered in March 1959 to Armadores de Cabotaje. She remained in this company's ownership until meeting her end after she stranded in bad weather three miles south of Valencia on 29 December 1980 when on passage from Barcelona to Algiers. She was subsequently demolished in situ.

(The late Peter Townsend, World Ship Photo Library)

We have only a limited selection of Spanish-built vessels to view but our second one is of considerable interest. The **Cap Maleas** (PAN, 1071grt/58) was built at the Astano shipyard in El Ferrol as the dry cargo ship **Maypa**. She was launched on 13 June 1957 and handed over in May of the following year. There are reports that under this name she and three sister vessels delivered weapons to dissident factions in East Pakistan, later to become Bangladesh, with only the **Maypa** returning to Spain. In 1961 she was renamed **Cibeles** and in late 1964 began to be converted to a liquefied gas tanker specifically for the carriage of butane. In 1967, she was renamed **Isla de Mouro** and became **Cap Maleas** following sale to Panamanian-flag operators in 1974. Our photograph shows her at anchor in Piraeus Roads on a hazy and scorching hot 8 August 1984. She had arrived from Algiers on 28 May 1984 and was laid up. She did not leave the area for later in the year she made the short voyage to Eleusis where she was demolished.

(Bernard McCall)

We have two examples of ships built in Italy and they were built at the same yard, namely the Giuliano shipyard in Trieste. The **Magdala** (ITA, 1594grt/55) was launched on 23 January 1955 and was completed in May 1955. Remaining in Italian ownership throughout her career, she was renamed **Mare Bianco** in 1976 and **Isola Bianca** in 1984. She was scrapped at Naples, arriving there for demolition in September 1986 after being laid up at Augusta since July 1985. She was photographed as she passed through the 90' Cutting on the Manchester Ship Canal on 20 August 1975.

(John Slavin)

The **Nha Rong 09** (VNM, 875gt/58) was photographed in Singapore Roads on 16 June 1998. Launched as **Laspeed**, she entered service as **Nhut Le** and was later renamed **Vam Co 24**. No dates are available for these changes of identity, but we know that she was eventually renamed **Huam Luyen 04** and she kept this name until 1994 when she became **Nha Rong 09** in the ownership of the mysteriously named Nha Rong Amphibious Transport Co. She remains in service in 2008, having been renamed **Khanh Long** in April 2006.

(Nigel Jones)

The **Eleni II** (GRC, 904grt/56) was photographed at Plymouth on 21 October 1973. She is our solitary example of a coaster built in a French yard, this being Société Anonyme des Anciens Chantiers Dubigeon in Nantes where she was launched on 26 June 1956. She was delivered to Norwegian owners as **Nicoto** in August 1956, and, still in Norwegian ownership, became **Jomara** in May 1963. Acquired by West German owners in 1965, she was renamed **Edda** and one source notes that she was converted to an open shelterdeck vessel with gross tonnage reduced to 496grt. Registers, however, continued to quote her original gross tonnage figure throughout her later career. In 1968 she was sold to Greek owners based in Heraklion and was renamed **Eleni II**, becoming **Lui** in July 1975. She was laid up at Piraeus in early November 1977 and was reported to have been scrapped there by late 1979.

(The late Peter Townsend, Ron Baker collection)

The **J. Caric** (HRV, 124gt/52) will certainly be an unfamiliar vessel to readers in north-west Europe. She was photographed at Supetar on the island of Brac in Croatia on 14 September 2007. She was built at the Brodogradiliste "Vicko Krstulovic" shipyard at Split in what is now Croatia but was once in Yugoslavia. Originally named **PB 32**, she became **Juraj Caric** in 1972. She remains listed under this name in *Lloyd's Register* which also notes that she has two 1-tonne derricks. At some stage, these have evidently been removed and replaced by a grab crane. As could be expected, she works in the local aggregates trades.

(David Oldham)

The **Agios Constantinos** (GRC, 459grt/57) is another coaster to illustrate the fact that some once-splendid vessels sometimes suffer a slow and sad decline. She has some significance within the context of this book, however, because she is the only representative of a ship built at a yard in Finland. She was built at Nystad by Nystads Varv Ab. This is the Swedish version of her builder's name which is identified in Finnish as Uudenkaupungin Telakka Oy, at Uusikaupunki. The yard was opened by the Erikson family in 1922, although other shipbuilding had been undertaken on the site since 1892. It was sold to Rauma-Repola in 1973.

Originally named **Fiskö** under the Finnish flag, after thirteen years service this refrigerated vessel was sold to Greek operators and was renamed **Koutouriaris S. IV**, later becoming **Glafki** between 1985 and 1988. It was then that she was renamed **Agios Constantinos**. By May 1990, she was reported to be laid up with damage and she did not trade again. She was towed to Ambelaki, Salamis, on 6 June 1990 and was photographed there on 6 October 2004. She is understood to have been scrapped in the Piraeus area in 2007.

(David Oldham)